بِسْمِ اللّٰه

In the name of Allah

This
BOOK
BELONGS to

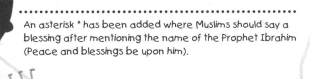

An asterisk * has been added where Muslims should say a blessing after mentioning the name of the Prophet Ibrahim (Peace and blessings be upon him).

Prophet Ibrahim and the Little Bird Activity Book

Published in 2020 by THE ISLAMIC FOUNDATION
An imprint OF KUBE PUBLISHING LTD
Tel: +44 (0)1530 249230
E-mail: info@kubepublishing.com
Website: www.kubepublishing.com

Text and illustrations © Ana Muslim Sdn Bhd, 2018
First published in Malaysia by Ana Muslim Sdn Bhd, 2017

• Writer: Saadah Taib
• Editor: Amalina Aida Abdul Rahim
• Illustrator: Shazana Rosli
• Cover design: Hazwanulhassan Mohd Nor
• Layout: Tan Peng Peng

A Cataloguing-in-Publication Data record for this book is available from the British Library

ISBN 978-0-86037-740-5
Printed by Omur, Turkey.

The Determined Little Bird

A long time ago, there was a small and timid bird. Yet, in spite of that, it acted tenaciously to save Prophet Ibrahim* from a very cruel king.

Prophet Ibrahim* was the Messenger of Allah.
He lived in a land ruled by a cruel king named
Namrud. Namrud burned Prophet Ibrahim* alive
because the prophet asked the king to worship
Allah.

The Little Bird Put Out the Flame

The little bird felt sorry for Prophet Ibrahim*.

Start

Help the little bird find its way to the fire.

It flew from one place to another looking for water to put out the fire that was burning Prophet Ibrahim*.

The little bird filled its beak with as much water as possible.

End

The Little Bird Was Mocked

The other birds made a mockery of the little bird. "It's useless. The water that you are carrying is too little. It will not be able to put out the huge flames."

Even though the little bird was mocked, it continued its effort to put out the fire.

Start

The little bird has to put out the fire as fast as possible. Help it find the path that leads to the water.

Sincere Help

The little bird did not know if its effort would pay off. But it was happy that it had tried its best to help.

"O Allah The All-Seeing and The All-Hearing. This is the only help that I can offer to Prophet Ibrahim*," said the little bird as it flew towards the burning flames.

Connect the dots.
What do you see? Colour it.

The Flames Died Down

Allah helped the little bird that sincerely tried to help Prophet Ibrahim*. By Allah's will, the fire slowly subsided.

Circle the shadows that look the same.

When the flames went out, many people came close to the bonfire. They thought that Prophet Ibrahim* had died.

Prophet Ibrahim*
Was Safe and Sound

Masha-Allah! All of them were shocked to see Prophet Ibrahim* walked out of the fire without any burns.

Alhamdulillah! The little bird was very happy. It knew that the fire did not go out because of the water that it brought, but because of the will and blessing of Allah.

Find these objects and circle them

The Little Bird Thanked Allah

The little bird flew away happily. It felt grateful to Allah that it was able to help Prophet Ibrahim*.

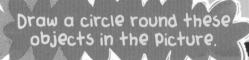
Draw a circle round these objects in the picture.

Dear friends, we should also remember to work hard at everything. Let's start with small things and try to keep doing them regularly.

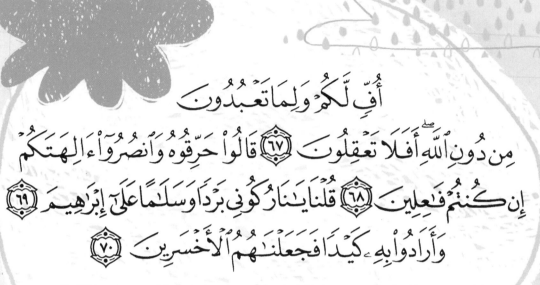

أُفٍّ لَّكُمْ وَلِمَا تَعْبُدُونَ مِن دُونِ ٱللَّهِ أَفَلَا تَعْقِلُونَ ۝ قَالُوا۟ حَرِّقُوهُ وَٱنصُرُوٓا۟ ءَالِهَتَكُمْ إِن كُنتُمْ فَاعِلِينَ ۝ قُلْنَا يَـٰنَارُ كُونِى بَرْدًا وَسَلَـٰمًا عَلَىٰٓ إِبْرَٰهِيمَ ۝ وَأَرَادُوا۟ بِهِۦ كَيْدًا فَجَعَلْنَـٰهُمُ ٱلْأَخْسَرِينَ ۝

"Uff to you and to what you worship instead of Allah.
Then will you not use reason?" They said, "Burn him and
support your gods - if you are to act."
Allah said, "O fire, be cool and provide safety upon
Ibrahim." And they intended for him harm, but
We made them the greatest losers.

(Surah Al-Anbya: 67-70)